con

M000078927

2–3
get it right – first time

4–31
recipes

32–33
get saucy!

34–59
recipes

60–61
glossary

62
index

63
facts and figures

British & North American Readers:
Please note that Australian cup and
spoon measurements are metric. A quick
conversion guide appears on page 63.
A glossary explaining unfamiliar terms
and ingredients begins on page 60.

2 get it right – **first** time

*If you've never tried filleting a fish, for example, it can seem
a little tricky. Here, we demystify some simple seafood-preparation
techniques so you can proceed with confidence.*

Filleting a round fish (such as bream or snapper)

1 Cut halfway through
fish along front fin.

2 Starting at head of
fish, cut flat against
spine; move knife
along spine towards
tail with a gentle press-
and-push motion.

3 This photo shows
the rib cage and fillet
cut away. Turn fish
over and repeat on
other side.

Skinning fillets

Cut a little of the flesh
from the skin at tail
end of fillet. Hold
the skin with salted
fingers (to aid grip) at
tail end and continue
cutting away flesh,
keeping knife flat
against the skin.

Shelling prawns and scampi

Note: some recipes require the head and tail, or just the tail, to remain intact. The same method is used whether they are cooked or uncooked, and whether it is prawns or scampi you are shelling.

1 To remove head, hold head firmly and twist body of prawn.

2 Remove legs and shell from body without removing tail shell.

3 To remove tail, first break off the two tail fins.

4 Slip tail shell from prawn.

5 Remove back vein from prawn (even if head and tail remain intact).

Butterflying garfish and sardines

1 Cut off head and remove entrails. Cut through underside to backbone; rinse under cold water.

2 Cut through backbone at tail end without piercing skin. Pull backbone out towards head end.

3 Remove small bones. This photo shows butterflied fish with bones removed.

4 cajun seafood
kebabs with avocado salsa

36 medium uncooked prawns (1kg)

800g firm white boneless fish fillets

2 tablespoons cajun seasoning

2 teaspoons ground cumin

2 tablespoons finely chopped fresh oregano

2 cloves garlic, crushed

1/4 cup (60ml) olive oil

avocado salsa

3 medium tomatoes (570g), seeded, chopped finely

1 small red onion (100g), chopped finely

1 large avocado (320g), chopped finely

2 tablespoons finely chopped fresh coriander

2 tablespoons lemon juice

1 tablespoon olive oil

1/2 teaspoon sugar

Shell and devein prawns, leaving tails intact. Cut fish into 3cm cubes.

Combine prawns and fish in large bowl with remaining ingredients, cover; refrigerate at least 20 minutes or until required.

Thread prawns and fish onto 12 skewers. Cook skewers on heated oiled barbecue, uncovered, until just cooked though. Serve with avocado salsa.

Avocado Salsa Combine ingredients in medium bowl.

SERVES 6
Per serving
24.3g fat; 1758kJ

6 oysters
with bacon butter

90g butter, softened

1 tablespoon
tomato sauce

1 tablespoon
worcestershire sauce

2 tablespoons finely
chopped fresh
flat-leaf parsley

2 bacon rashers
(140g), chopped finely

24 medium oysters
(1.5kg), on the
half shell

Beat butter in small bowl until smooth; stir in
sauces and parsley. Cook bacon on heated
oiled barbecue plate, stirring, until crisp;
drain on absorbent paper. Stir bacon into
butter mixture; refrigerate until firm.
Place a heaped teaspoon of bacon butter
onto each oyster; cook on heated barbecue
until butter is melted.

SERVES 4
Per serving 24.6g fat; 1292kJ

crab and zucchini
fritters

3/4 cup (110g) self-raising flour

1 egg

1 cup (250ml) milk

2 green onions, chopped finely

8 crab sticks (250g), chopped finely

1 medium zucchini (120g), grated coarsely

2 tablespoons coarsely chopped fresh coriander

Place flour in large bowl, gradually stir in combined egg and milk; mix to a smooth batter. Stir in onion, crab, zucchini and coriander.
Spoon level tablespoons of mixture onto heated oiled barbecue plate; cook, uncovered, until browned lightly on both sides.

MAKES 25
Per serving 0.8g fat; 144kJ

balmain bugs
with oregano

16 medium uncooked balmain bugs (1.8kg), halved, cleaned

¼ cup (60ml) dry white wine

¼ cup (60ml) lime juice

¼ cup (60ml) olive oil

2 tablespoons finely chopped fresh oregano

2 cloves garlic, crushed

Combine bugs in large bowl with remaining ingredients, cover; refrigerate at least 20 minutes or until required.

Drain bugs over small bowl; reserve marinade. Cook bugs on heated oiled barbecue, uncovered, brushing occasionally with reserved marinade, until just changed in colour.

SERVES 4
Per serving 17g fat; 2052kJ

10 salmon cutlets
with creamy dill sauce

6 medium potatoes
(1.2kg), sliced thickly

4 salmon cutlets (1kg)

500g asparagus,
trimmed

creamy dill sauce

300ml thickened
light cream

$1/4$ cup (60ml) dry
white wine

2 cloves garlic,
crushed

3 green onions,
chopped finely

2 tablespoons finely
chopped fresh dill

Boil, steam or microwave potato until almost tender. Cook salmon and potato on heated oiled barbecue, uncovered, until salmon is cooked as desired and potato is browned both sides and tender. Cook asparagus on heated oiled barbecue, uncovered, until just tender. Serve salmon, potato and asparagus with creamy dill sauce.

Creamy Dill Sauce Combine cream, wine, garlic and onion in medium frying pan, place on barbecue; simmer, uncovered, until sauce thickens slightly. Remove pan from heat, stir in dill.

SERVES 4
Per serving 17.1g fat; 2514kJ

coconut prawns
with coriander mayonnaise

30 large uncooked
prawns (1.5kg)

2 eggs, beaten lightly

3/4 cup (50g)
shredded coconut

**coriander
mayonnaise**

1/4 teaspoon
ground turmeric

2 tablespoons
boiling water

1/2 cup (150g)
mayonnaise

2 tablespoons
finely chopped
fresh coriander

1 clove garlic, crushed

2 teaspoons finely
grated lemon rind

Shell and devein prawns, leaving tails intact.
Dip prawns in egg, coat in coconut, place on
tray, cover; refrigerate 20 minutes.
Cook prawns on heated oiled barbecue plate,
uncovered, until browned lightly both sides and
just changed in colour. Serve with coriander
mayonnaise and barbecued roti, if desired.
Coriander Mayonnaise Blend turmeric with the
water in small bowl. Stir in remaining ingredients.

SERVES 6
Per serving 16g fat; 1170kJ

12 devilled squid

2 large squid
hoods (400g)

$1/4$ cup finely chopped
fresh mint

marinade

2 teaspoons finely
grated lemon rind

$1/4$ cup (60ml)
lemon juice

1 tablespoon
peanut oil

2 cloves garlic,
crushed

2 teaspoons
Tabasco sauce

lime vinaigrette

2 teaspoons sugar

2 tablespoons
lime juice

$1/3$ cup (80ml)
peanut oil

2 cloves garlic,
crushed

2 green onions,
chopped finely

1 red thai chilli,
sliced thinly

Cut squid hoods in half lengthways, then
cut lengthways into 1cm strips; thread onto
12 skewers. Combine squid skewers with
marinade in large shallow dish, cover;
refrigerate at least 20 minutes or until required.
Drain squid skewers over small bowl; reserve
marinade. Cook squid skewers on heated oiled
barbecue, uncovered, brushing occasionally
with reserved marinade, until browned lightly
and tender. Serve sprinkled with mint; serve
with lime vinaigrette.
Marinade Combine ingredients in small bowl.
Lime Vinaigrette Combine ingredients in
screw-top jar; shake well.

SERVES 4
Per serving 24.2g fat; 1266kJ

teriyaki snapper
with soba

½ cup (125ml)
light soy sauce

¼ cup (60ml)
oyster sauce

2 tablespoons
brown sugar

¼ cup (60ml)
mirin

4 thick snapper
steaks (800g)

250g packet
soba noodles

Combine sauces, sugar and mirin in large bowl; add fish.
Cover; refrigerate at least 20 minutes or until required.
Drain fish over small saucepan; reserve marinade. Cook fish
on heated oiled barbecue, uncovered, until browned both
sides and just cooked through.
Meanwhile, place reserved marinade on barbecue, bring to
a boil; simmer, uncovered, 2 minutes. Cook noodles according
to directions on packet; drain. Stir marinade through noodles.
Serve fish on top of noodles.

SERVES 4
Per serving 4.1g fat; 1978kJ

14 seafood **corn** husks

Remove corn cobs carefully from husks, keeping husks intact at base. Remove silk from husks. Trim ends neatly from husks.

Combine prawns with scallops, butter, parsley and juice in medium bowl. Fill husks with seafood mixture; tie ends of husks with strips of husks.

Cook seafood husks on heated oil barbecue, uncovered, brushing occasionally with oil, until browned and heated through.

Meanwhile, cut corn from cobs; boil, steam or microwave until just tender, drain. Combine corn with remaining ingredients in medium bowl. Serve seafood corn husks with corn salad.

6 corn cobs in husks (2.4kg)

500g shelled cooked prawns

250g scallops

60g butter, melted

2 tablespoons finely chopped fresh flat-leaf parsley

2 tablespoons lemon juice

2 tablespoons vegetable oil

1 medium red capsicum (200g), chopped finely

4 green onions, sliced thinly

1/4 cup coarsely chopped fresh coriander

1 medium red onion (170g), chopped finely

2 tablespoons lime juice

SERVES 6
Per serving 19.3g fat; 2244kJ

1 teaspoon
chilli powder

1 tablespoon
garlic salt

2 tablespoons
dried oregano

2 tablespoons
dried thyme

2 teaspoons
sweet paprika

4 orange roughy
fillets (1kg)

30g butter, melted

1 clove garlic, crushed

1 tablespoon olive oil

4 corn tortillas

fresh salsa

4 medium tomatoes
(760g), seeded,
chopped finely

1 small red onion
(100g), chopped finely

1 tablespoon olive oil

1 tablespoon
finely chopped
fresh oregano

Combine chilli powder, salt, oregano, thyme and
paprika in small bowl. Brush fish all over with
butter; coat with spice mixture.

Cook fish on heated oiled barbecue, uncovered,
until browned both sides and just cooked through.
Cover to keep warm.

Place garlic in small bowl with oil; brush oil mixture
over both sides of each tortilla. Place tortillas on
oven tray; bake, uncovered, in hot oven 5 minutes
or until crisp. Cut each tortilla into eight pieces.
Serve fish with tortilla triangles and fresh salsa.

Fresh Salsa Combine ingredients in medium bowl.

SERVES 4
Per serving 24.6g fat; 2225kJ

16 black bean and
chilli prawn kebabs

36 medium uncooked
prawns (1kg), shelled

1½ tablespoons salted
black beans, drained,
rinsed, chopped finely

1 clove garlic, crushed

2 teaspoons grated
fresh ginger

1 tablespoon
dry sherry

2 tablespoons light
soy sauce

1 teaspoon sesame oil

1 red thai chilli,
chopped finely

⅓ cup (80ml) light
soy sauce, extra

Combine prawns, beans, garlic, ginger, sherry,
sauce, oil and chilli in large bowl, cover;
refrigerate at least 20 minutes or until required.
Thread prawns onto 12 skewers. Cook kebabs
on heated oiled barbecue, uncovered, until
browned all over and just changed in colour.
Serve with extra soy sauce.

SERVES 4
Per serving 2.2g fat; 624kJ

flathead fillets with
tarragon butter

1 large kumara (500g)

12 flathead
fillets (600g)

2 tablespoons
plain flour

salt and pepper

150g baby
green beans

150g snow peas

100g sugar snap peas

50g butter, melted

1 tablespoon
coarsely chopped
fresh tarragon

Cut the kumara into 2cm thick slices. Boil, steam or microwave kumara until just tender; drain.

Toss fish fillets in combined flour, salt and pepper; shake off excess. Cook fish and kumara on heated oiled barbecue, uncovered, until fish is browned both sides and just cooked through and kumara is browned both sides.

Meanwhile, boil, steam or microwave beans and peas until just tender; drain.

Divide kumara among serving plates, top with beans, peas and fish. Drizzle with combined butter and tarragon.

SERVES 4
Per serving 14g fat; 1598kJ

18 spiced snapper
with nutty rice

You will need about ²/₃ cup (130g) uncooked medium-grain white rice for this recipe.

2 tablespoons
ground coriander

1 tablespoon ground cumin

2 teaspoons mustard powder

2 teaspoons sweet paprika

¹/₃ cup (80ml) peanut oil

2kg whole snapper

seasoning

60g butter

1 medium brown onion
(150g), chopped finely

2 cloves garlic, crushed

2 teaspoons mild
curry powder

2 cups cooked white rice

¹/₂ cup (75g) coarsely
chopped shelled
pistachios, toasted

2 tablespoons finely
chopped fresh
flat-leaf parsley

2 tablespoons finely
chopped fresh coriander

2 teaspoons finely
grated lemon rind

Cook ground spices
in small frying pan,
stirring, until fragrant,
cool; stir in oil.
Cut fish three times on
each side. Place fish on
a large sheet of oiled
foil. Fill fish cavity with
seasoning; brush fish all
over with spice mixture.
Seal foil to enclose fish.
Cook fish on heated
oiled barbecue, turning
occasionally, until fish
is just cooked through.
Seasoning Heat butter
in small saucepan; cook
onion, garlic and curry
powder, stirring, until
onion is soft. Combine
onion mixture with
remaining ingredients
in medium bowl.

SERVES 6
Per serving
29.5g fat; 2021kJ

20 baby octopus salad

Remove and discard heads and beaks from octopus; cut each octopus in half. Using a vegetable peeler, remove five wide strips of rind from lemon; shred strips finely.
Combine octopus, rind, garlic, paprika, cumin, pesto, vinegar and half of the oil in large bowl; cover, refrigerate at least 20 minutes or until required.
Drain octopus over small saucepan; reserve marinade. Cook octopus on heated oiled barbecue, uncovered, until tender; place in large heatproof bowl, cover to keep warm. Bring marinade to a boil; pour over octopus.
Cut tomatoes into thin wedges; add to octopus with rocket, spinach, onion, cheese and olives, mix gently.
Combine juice with remaining oil in small jug; drizzle over octopus salad.

SERVES 4
Per serving 31g fat; 2127kJ

1.5kg baby octopus

1 medium lemon (140g)

4 cloves garlic, crushed

1 teaspoon hot paprika

1 teaspoon ground cumin

2 tablespoons bottled basil pesto

1/4 cup (60ml) balsamic vinegar

1/3 cup (80ml) olive oil

2 medium tomatoes (380g)

250g baby rocket, trimmed

100g baby spinach leaves, trimmed

1 medium red onion (170g), sliced thinly

100g fetta, chopped coarsely

1/2 cup (40g) seeded black olives

2 tablespoons lemon juice

40 small black
mussels (1kg)

80g butter

2 tablespoons
drained canned
green peppercorns,
chopped coarsely

2 teaspoons finely
grated lemon rind

1/4 cup finely chopped
fresh flat-leaf parsley

Scrub mussels, remove beards. Cook mussels
in large saucepan of boiling water, uncovered,
until mussels open (discard any that do not).
Remove and discard half of each shell.
Spread combined butter, peppercorns and
rind evenly over mussel meat in each shell.
Cook mussels, uncovered, on heated
barbecue until heated through. Just before
serving, sprinkle with parsley.

SERVES 4
Per serving 18.1g fat; 966kJ

3 medium
potatoes (600g)

2 medium
lemons (280g)

2 pickled baby
dill cucumbers,
sliced thinly

4 tuna steaks (800g)

2 teaspoons drained
canned green
peppercorns

2 teaspoons drained
tiny capers

Boil, steam or microwave potatoes until just tender; cut each potato
into four slices. Cut each lemon into six slices. Cook lemon, potato and
cucumber on heated oiled barbecue, uncovered, until just tender, cover
to keep warm. Cook tuna on heated oiled barbecue, uncovered, until
browned both sides and cooked as desired. Heat peppercorns and
capers on barbecue plate until hot.
Divide potato among plates, then top with tuna, lemon and cucumber.
Sprinkle with peppercorns and capers.

SERVES 4
Per serving 11.7g fat; 1764kJ

blue-eye with lemon
and garlic

4 blue-eye
cutlets (1kg)

16 packaged vine
leaves in brine

2 medium lemons
(280g), sliced thinly

2 tablespoons olive oil

2 cloves garlic, crushed

2 tablespoons dry
white wine

Centre each piece of fish on four vine leaves, top with lemon slices; drizzle with combined oil, garlic and wine; wrap vine leaves to enclose fish. Place each parcel of fish on a large sheet of oiled foil. Seal foil to enclose fish.
Cook parcels on heated oiled barbecue until fish is just cooked through.

SERVES 4
Per serving 13.7g fat; 1301kJ

24

squid and
watercress
salad

1kg squid hoods

1½ teaspoons
ground cumin

2 tablespoons finely
chopped fresh dill

2 tablespoons
lemon juice

2 tablespoons
barbecue sauce

¼ cup (60ml) sweet
chilli sauce

¼ cup (60ml)
peanut oil

1 tablespoon finely
grated lemon rind

2 cloves garlic,
crushed

2 lebanese
cucumbers (260g)

1 medium red
capsicum (200g),
sliced thinly

140g watercress

1 tablespoon water

Cut squid in half lengthways, score inside surface of each piece; cut diagonally into 2cm-wide strips.

Combine cumin, dill, juice, sauces and oil in small jug; mix well.

Combine squid, rind and garlic in large bowl with half of the cumin mixture; cover, refrigerate at least 20 minutes or until required. Cover remaining cumin mixture; refrigerate until required.

Drain squid; discard marinade. Cook squid on heated oiled barbecue, uncovered, until tender and browned all over, cover to keep warm.

Halve cucumbers lengthways; cut into thin slices. Combine cucumber with capsicum and watercress in large bowl.

Stir the water into reserved cumin mixture; pour over salad, toss gently to combine. Serve squid with salad.

SERVES 4
Per serving 17.5g fat; 1563kJ

26 fish steak with
tomato and chilli butter

6 swordfish
steaks (1.2kg)

1 teaspoon finely
grated lime rind

1/4 cup (60ml)
lime juice

**tomato and
chilli butter**

125g butter

1/3 cup (50g) finely
chopped, drained
sun-dried tomatoes
in oil

1 tablespoon
lime juice

1 tablespoon
sambal oelek

1 tablespoon finely
chopped fresh
flat-leaf parsley

2 green onions,
chopped finely

Combine fish with rind and juice in large
bowl, cover; refrigerate at least 20 minutes
or until required.

Drain fish; discard marinade. Cook fish on
heated oiled barbecue, uncovered, until
browned both sides and just cooked through.
Serve fish with tomato and chilli butter, and
crusty bread and spinach, if desired.

Tomato and Chilli Butter Beat butter in small
bowl with electric mixer until light and fluffy;
stir in remaining ingredients. Spoon mixture
onto piece of foil, roll up firmly; shape into
a log, freeze until firm.

SERVES 6
Per serving 22.3g fat; 1612kJ

garlic prawns with
tomato sauce

24 large uncooked prawns (1.2kg)

2 cloves garlic, crushed

2 tablespoons olive oil

4 green onions

tomato sauce

3/4 cup (180ml) tomato puree

1 red thai chilli, chopped finely

1 tablespoon brown vinegar

1/2 cup (125ml) vegetable stock

2 tablespoons finely chopped fresh flat-leaf parsley

1 tablespoon finely chopped fresh oregano

Shell and devein prawns, leaving tails intact. Combine prawns, garlic and oil in medium bowl, cover; refrigerate at least 20 minutes or until required. Cut onions into strips. Wrap an onion strip around each prawn; thread prawns onto eight skewers.

Cook skewers on heated oiled barbecue, uncovered, until browned lightly and just changed in colour; serve with tomato sauce.

Tomato Sauce Combine puree, chilli, vinegar and stock in small frying pan, place on barbecue; simmer, uncovered, until thickened slightly. Remove pan from heat; stir in herbs.

SERVES 4
Per serving 10.2g fat; 984kJ

fish cutlets with
salsa

2 lebanese cucumbers
(260g), seeded,
chopped finely

2 medium radishes
(70g), chopped finely

4 medium egg
tomatoes (300g),
seeded, chopped
finely

1 medium yellow
capsicum (200g),
seeded, chopped
finely

1/2 teaspoon
Tabasco sauce

1 tablespoon
sherry vinegar

4 white fish cutlets
(1kg), bones removed

Combine cucumber, radish, tomato, capsicum,
sauce and vinegar in medium bowl.
Cook fish on heated oiled barbecue, uncovered,
until browned both sides and just cooked
through. Serve fish with salsa.

SERVES 4
Per serving 5.3g fat; 1113kJ

sardines with

tomatoes and caper dressing

12 whole sardines (750g), cleaned

4 medium egg tomatoes (300g), sliced thickly

1 small red onion (100g), sliced thinly

1 tablespoon flat-leaf parsley leaves

caper dressing

1/3 cup (80ml) red wine vinegar

1/4 cup (60ml) olive oil

1 tablespoon drained tiny capers

1 clove garlic, crushed

1 tablespoon coarsely chopped fresh flat-leaf parsley

Remove and discard sardine heads. To butterfly sardines, cut through the underside of fish to the tail. Break backbone at the tail; peel away backbone, trim fish. (Also see page 3.)
Cook sardines on heated oiled barbecue, uncovered, until browned both sides and just cooked through. Serve with tomato and onion; spoon over caper dressing, sprinkle with parsley.
Caper Dressing Combine ingredients in screw-top jar; shake well.

SERVES 4
Per serving 16.3g fat; 1138kJ

with two sauces

1.2kg side of salmon

1 tablespoon coarse cooking salt

dill caper cream

1²/₃ cups (400g) low-fat sour cream

2 tablespoons finely chopped fresh dill

1 small red onion (100g), chopped finely

¹/₄ cup (60g) drained capers, chopped coarsely

preserved-lemon yogurt

400g low-fat yogurt

¹/₄ cup (60g) finely chopped preserved lemons

1 tablespoon finely chopped fresh coriander

1 tablespoon finely chopped fresh mint

2 cloves garlic, crushed

Remove any bones from salmon. Rub salt into skin; cook, skin-side down, on heated oiled barbecue, uncovered, 10 minutes. Turn salmon; cook 5 minutes or until cooked as desired. Cut salmon into six pieces crossways; serve with sauces.
Dill Caper Cream Combine ingredients in small bowl.
Preserved-Lemon Yogurt Combine ingredients in small bowl.

SERVES 6
Per serving 27.4g fat; 1983kJ

basil prawns

with avocado mash

1kg medium uncooked prawns

½ cup finely chopped fresh basil

2 cloves garlic, crushed

1 tablespoon finely grated lime rind

2 tablespoons peanut oil

avocado mash

2 medium avocados (500g)

2 tablespoons lime juice

2 medium tomatoes (380g), seeded, chopped finely

1 small red onion (100g), chopped finely

2 teaspoons ground cumin

2 tablespoons finely chopped fresh basil

1 red thai chilli, seeded, chopped finely

Shell and devein prawns, leaving tails intact. Combine prawns in large bowl with remaining ingredients, cover; refrigerate at least 20 minutes or until required.

Cook prawns on heated oiled barbecue, uncovered, until browned and changed in colour. Serve prawns with avocado mash.

Avocado Mash Mash flesh of one avocado in medium bowl until almost smooth. Chop flesh of remaining avocado roughly; add to mashed avocado with remaining ingredients, mix well.

SERVES 4
Per serving 30g fat; 1689kJ

32 get saucy!

The subtle taste of fresh seafood is all the more scrumptious when accompanied by a riotous hit of flavour. These four easy sauces will transform any seafood you serve into the simply spectacular.

chilli ginger dipping sauce

1/3 cup (80ml) chicken stock

2 teaspoons grated fresh ginger

1 tablespoon dried crushed chillies

2 tablespoons light soy sauce

2 teaspoons dry sherry

2 tablespoons finely chopped fresh coriander

Combine ingredients in small bowl.

MAKES 1/2 cup (125ml)
Per tablespoon 0.3g fat; 44kJ

thousand island dressing

1/2 cup (150g) mayonnaise

1/3 cup (80ml) tomato sauce

1/4 teaspoon Tabasco sauce

2 teaspoons worcestershire sauce

1 teaspoon dijon mustard

Combine ingredients in small bowl.

MAKES 3/4 cup (180ml)
Per tablespoon 5.4g fat; 300kJ

dill and caper mayonnaise

2 egg yolks

1 tablespoon lemon juice

2 teaspoons dijon mustard

1 cup (250ml) vegetable oil

1 tablespoon drained capers, chopped coarsely

1 tablespoon finely chopped fresh dill

1 tablespoon finely grated lemon rind

Blend or process egg yolks, juice and mustard until smooth. With motor operating, gradually pour in oil; process until thick. Stir in capers, dill and rind.

MAKES 1½ cups (375ml)
Per tablespoon 13.4g fat; 507kJ

creamy avocado sauce

1 large avocado (320g)

¼ cup (60g) sour cream

¼ cup (75g) mayonnaise

2 tablespoons olive oil

1 teaspoon Tabasco sauce

1 clove garlic, crushed

¼ cup tightly packed fresh coriander

1 tablespoon lemon juice

Blend or process ingredients until smooth.

MAKES 1½ cups (375ml)
Per tablespoon 5.5g fat; 228kJ

34 walnut gremolata
bream

1/3 cup (35g) walnut pieces, toasted, chopped finely

2 tablespoons finely chopped lemon rind

1/4 cup finely chopped fresh flat-leaf parsley

2 cloves garlic, crushed

4 medium potatoes (800g), quartered

40g butter, chopped coarsely

1/4 cup (60ml) milk

4 bream fillets (800g)

1 tablespoon olive oil

Combine nuts, rind, parsley and half of the garlic in small bowl; cover gremolata.

Boil, steam or microwave potato until tender; drain. Mash potato with butter, milk and remaining garlic.

Meanwhile, brush fish with oil; cook, skin-side down first, on heated oiled barbecue, until browned both sides and cooked through.

Serve fish on garlic mash; sprinkle with gremolata.

SERVES 4
Per serving 29.9g fat; 2367kJ

octopus

1.25kg baby octopus

2 tablespoons sweet chilli sauce

1 tablespoon kecap manis

$1/4$ cup (60ml) lime juice

2 cloves garlic, crushed

2 tablespoons finely chopped fresh coriander

2 medium limes (160g), sliced thickly

Remove and discard heads and beaks from octopus; cut each octopus in half.

Combine octopus with sauce, kecap manis, juice, garlic and coriander in large bowl, cover; refrigerate at least 20 minutes or until required.

Drain octopus; discard marinade. Cook octopus and lime slices on heated oiled barbecue, uncovered, until octopus is browned and tender and lime slices are browned both sides.

SERVES 4
Per serving 2.6g fat; 708kJ

36 prawn kebabs
with chilli lime sauce

32 medium
uncooked
prawns (800g)

2 cloves garlic,
crushed

1 tablespoon finely
chopped fresh
lemon grass

1 tablespoon
balsamic vinegar

1 tablespoon
coarsely chopped
fresh coriander

1 tablespoon
peanut oil

4 green onions

chilli lime sauce

²/₃ cup (150g)
sugar

¹/₂ cup (125ml)
water

1 teaspoon finely
grated lime rind

2 red thai
chillies, seeded,
chopped finely

2 tablespoons
sweet chilli sauce

¹/₃ cup (80ml)
lime juice

Shell and devein prawns, leaving tails intact.
Combine prawns in medium bowl with garlic,
lemon grass, vinegar, coriander and oil, cover;
refrigerate at least 20 minutes or until required.
Drain prawns; discard marinade. Cut onions into
5cm lengths; alternating onion pieces and prawns,
thread onto eight skewers. Cook on heated oiled
barbecue, uncovered, until browned both sides.
Serve kebabs with chilli lime sauce.
Chilli Lime Sauce Combine sugar and the water
in small saucepan; stir over heat, without boiling,
until sugar dissolves. Simmer, uncovered, without
stirring, 5 minutes. Add rind, chilli and sauce;
simmer, uncovered, 5 minutes. Stir in juice; cool.

SERVES 4
Per serving 5.3g fat; 1180kJ

fish cutlets with
artichoke

2/3 cup (180g) bottled basil pesto

1 cup firmly packed fresh basil leaves

2 x 400g cans artichoke hearts, drained, halved

1 large red onion (300g), sliced thinly

2 large mushrooms (300g), peeled, sliced thickly

2 baby eggplants (120g), sliced thinly lengthways

4 blue-eye cutlets (1kg)

1/2 cup firmly packed fresh basil leaves, extra

Blend or process pesto and basil until combined; reserve 1/4 cup pesto mixture.

Combine artichoke, onion, mushrooms, eggplant and half of the remaining pesto mixture in large bowl.

Cook vegetables and mushrooms on heated oiled barbecue plate, uncovered, until browned and tender; cover, keep warm. Brush fish with reserved 1/4 cup pesto mixture. Cook fish on heated oiled barbecue, uncovered, until cooked through.

Combine remaining pesto mixture, extra basil and barbecued vegetables in large bowl. Divide vegetables among serving plates; top with fish.

SERVES 4
Per serving 23.2g fat; 1894kJ

ginger tuna
with wasabi drizzle

1/3 cup (80ml)
olive oil

2 teaspoons grated
fresh ginger

2 red thai
chillies, seeded,
chopped finely

2 tablespoons finely
chopped fresh
lemon grass

4 thick tuna
steaks (800g)

wasabi drizzle

1 cup (250ml) dry
white wine

2 tablespoons finely
chopped palm sugar

1/3 cup (80ml)
cider vinegar

1 tablespoon wasabi

2/3 cup (160g) low-fat
sour cream

Combine oil, ginger, chilli and lemon grass
in large bowl; add tuna. Cover; refrigerate at
least 20 minutes or until required.

Drain tuna over small bowl; reserve marinade.
Cook tuna on heated oiled barbecue,
uncovered, brushing with reserved marinade,
until browned both sides and cooked as
desired. Serve with wasabi drizzle.

Wasabi Drizzle Combine wine, sugar and
vinegar in small saucepan, place on barbecue;
simmer, uncovered, until reduced by half, cool
slightly. Stir in wasabi and sour cream.

SERVES 4
Per serving 42.1g fat; 2711kJ

scampi with
fresh herbs

*12 uncooked
scampi (600g)*

90g butter, melted

2 tablespoons olive oil

*2 tablespoons finely
chopped fresh
flat-leaf parsley*

*2 tablespoons finely
chopped fresh coriander*

*2 tablespoons finely
chopped fresh basil*

*1 tablespoon finely
chopped fresh rosemary*

Cut scampi in half lengthways, leaving
shells intact. Clean heads and remove
vein along each back.

Toss scampi with half of the combined
butter and oil in large bowl. Add herbs
to remaining butter and oil.

Cook scampi on heated oiled barbecue,
uncovered, until changed in colour. Toss
hot scampi in large bowl with herb mixture.

SERVES 4
Per serving 28.5g fat; 1487kJ

salmon with kipfler
potatoes
and pesto mayonnaise

10 kipfler potatoes (500g)

1 cup firmly packed fresh basil

1 clove garlic, crushed

1 tablespoon pine nuts, toasted

1 tablespoon finely grated parmesan cheese

1/4 cup (60ml) olive oil

6 salmon fillets (1.2kg)

1/2 cup (150g) low-fat mayonnaise

Boil, steam or microwave potatoes until just tender; halve lengthways.

Blend or process basil, garlic, nuts, cheese and oil until almost smooth. Coat potatoes and salmon with 2 tablespoons of the pesto mixture, cover; refrigerate 10 minutes.

Meanwhile, combine remaining pesto mixture with mayonnaise in small bowl, press plastic wrap over surface of pesto mayonnaise.

Cook salmon and potatoes on heated oiled barbecue, uncovered, until salmon is browned both sides and cooked as desired and potatoes are browned; serve with pesto mayonnaise.

SERVES 4
Per serving 39.9g fat; 2658kJ

lemon and mustard
squid hoods

You will need about 1¹/₃ cups (265g) uncooked white rice for this recipe.

1 tablespoon olive oil

1 small white onion (80g), chopped finely

2 cloves garlic, crushed

4 green onions, chopped finely

4 cups cooked medium-grain white rice

¹/₂ cup (40g) finely grated fresh parmesan

1 tablespoon finely grated lemon rind

1 egg, beaten lightly

1 tablespoon mild english mustard

6 medium squid hoods (960g)

lemon and mustard dressing

¹/₃ cup (80ml) olive oil

1 clove garlic, crushed

2 tablespoons lemon juice

2 teaspoons mild english mustard

¹/₂ teaspoon sugar

Heat oil in small saucepan; cook white onion and garlic, stirring, until onion is soft. Add green onion; cook, stirring, until just soft.

Combine rice, onion mixture, cheese, rind, egg and mustard in large bowl.

Spoon mixture into squid hoods, securing ends with toothpicks; cook on heated oiled barbecue, uncovered, until browned all over and tender. Serve drizzled with lemon and mustard dressing.

Lemon and Mustard Dressing Combine ingredients in jar; shake well.

SERVES 4
Per serving
26.2g fat; 2850kJ

tuna steaks with olive and fetta salsa

1 tablespoon olive oil

1 tablespoon lemon juice

1/4 teaspoon cracked
black pepper

8 tuna steaks (1.6kg)

olive and fetta salsa

4 medium tomatoes (760g),
seeded, chopped finely

200g seeded black olives,
sliced thinly

300g fetta, chopped finely

1/3 cup finely chopped
fresh oregano

2 tablespoons pine
nuts, toasted

Combine oil, juice and pepper
in small jug; brush over tuna.
Cook tuna on heated oiled
barbecue, uncovered,
brushing occasionally with oil
mixture, until browned both
sides and cooked as desired.
Serve immediately with olive
and fetta salsa.
Olive and Fetta Salsa Combine
ingredients in medium bowl.

SERVES 8
Per serving 26.1g fat; 2096kJ

6 tuna steaks (1.2kg)

1/2 cup (125ml) olive oil

2 cloves garlic, crushed

1/4 cup (60ml) lemon juice

6 medium egg tomatoes (450g), halved

1/2 cup finely chopped fresh flat-leaf parsley

1/4 cup finely chopped fresh oregano

2 tablespoons finely grated lemon rind

1/3 cup (80g) drained capers, chopped coarsely

200g seeded kalamata olives, halved

Remove skin from tuna, place tuna in large bowl with oil, garlic and juice, cover; refrigerate at least 20 minutes or until required.
Drain tuna over medium bowl; reserve marinade. Cook tuna and tomatoes on heated oiled barbecue, uncovered, brushing occasionally with reserved marinade, until tuna is browned both sides and cooked as desired and tomatoes are browned and softened slightly.
Serve tuna with tomatoes, sprinkled with combined herbs, rind, capers and olives; serve with spinach, if desired.

SERVES 6
Per serving 30.2g fat; 2176kJ

chilli plum crabs

6 medium uncooked
blue swimmer
crabs (4.5kg)

¹/₂ cup (125ml)
plum sauce

2 tablespoons
oyster sauce

1 tablespoon light
soy sauce

1 clove garlic, crushed

1 tablespoon grated
fresh ginger

1 tablespoon
chilli sauce

2 tablespoons
peanut oil

¹/₂ teaspoon
sesame oil

¹/₂ cup (125ml) sweet
chilli sauce

To kill crabs humanely; drown in fresh water or freeze for 2 hours
(any longer will freeze the meat).

Hold crabs firmly. Slide sharp, strong knife under top of shell at back,
lever off shell. Remove and discard whitish gills. Rinse well under
cold water. Crack nippers slightly; cut crabs in half.

Combine crabs with remaining ingredients in large bowl, cover;
refrigerate at least 20 minutes or until required.

Cook undrained crabs on heated oiled barbecue, uncovered,
until changed in colour, turning occasionally.

SERVES 6
Per serving 9.5g fat; 1503kJ

46 garfish

with leek, prosciutto and prawns

1 medium leek (350g)

12 large cooked prawns (250g)

12 whole garfish (820g), butterflied (see page 3)

12 slices prosciutto (190g)

¼ cup (70g) roasted vegetable pesto

2 medium yellow zucchini (240g)

2 medium green zucchini (240g)

Cut leek in half lengthways; cut into 10cm lengths. Separate layers of leek. Immerse leek in boiling water, drain; rinse under cold water, drain. **Shell** and devein prawns, leaving tails intact.

Flatten one garfish with rolling pin, place fish, skin-side down, on board; line with pieces of leek then prosciutto. Spread with 1 teaspoon pesto, top with prawn. Starting from head of fish, roll to enclose prawn; secure with toothpick. Repeat with remaining ingredients.

Cut zucchini lengthways into 5mm-thick slices. Cook on heated oiled barbecue until browned and tender; cover, keep warm.

Cook fish on heated oiled barbecue until cooked through. Serve fish with char-grilled zucchini.

SERVES 4
Per serving 10g fat; 1246kJ

cumin fish cutlets with coriander chilli sauce

6 white fish
cutlets (1.5kg)

2 teaspoons
cumin seeds

**coriander
chilli sauce**

8 green onions,
chopped coarsely

3 cloves garlic,
quartered

2 red thai
chillies, seeded,
chopped coarsely

1 tablespoon
coarsely chopped
coriander root

2 tablespoons
brown sugar

2 tablespoons
fish sauce

1/4 cup (60ml)
lime juice

Sprinkle one side of each fish cutlet with
the seeds. Cook fish on heated oiled barbecue,
uncovered, until browned both sides and
just cooked through. Serve fish with coriander
chilli sauce.

Coriander Chilli Sauce Blend or process
onion, garlic, chilli, coriander root and sugar
until finely chopped. Add sauce and juice;
blend until combined.

SERVES 6
Per serving 5.3g fat; 1111kJ

40 medium uncooked prawns (1kg)

¹/₄ cup (60ml) peanut oil

2 cloves garlic, crushed

2 tablespoons sambal oelek

1¹/₂ tablespoons finely chopped fresh thyme

Shell and devein prawns, leaving heads and tails intact. Combine prawns with remaining ingredients in large bowl, cover; refrigerate at least 20 minutes or until required.
Cook prawns, uncovered, on heated oiled barbecue, until browned both sides and changed in colour.

SERVES 4
Per serving 14.7g fat; 1024kJ

50 blackened blue-eye
with sweet tomato relish

4 blue-eye fillets (800g)

2 tablespoons olive oil

2 tablespoons grated fresh ginger

1 1/2 tablespoons ground turmeric

1 tablespoon garlic powder

1 tablespoon mustard powder

1 tablespoon sweet paprika

1 tablespoon dried basil leaves

1 tablespoon ground fennel

1/4 teaspoon cayenne pepper

1/4 teaspoon chilli powder

sweet tomato relish

10 medium egg tomatoes
(750g), halved

2 cups (500ml) water

1/2 cup (125ml) dry white wine

1 tablespoon finely grated lime rind

1 tablespoon lime juice

1/2 cup (100g) firmly packed
brown sugar

1 tablespoon ground turmeric

1 tablespoon yellow mustard seeds

2 stalks fresh lemon grass

Place fish in large shallow dish; pour over combined oil and ginger. Cover; refrigerate at least 20 minutes or until required. Drain fish; discard marinade.
Coat fish in combined remaining ingredients; cook on heated oiled barbecue, uncovered, until browned both sides and just cooked through. Serve with sweet tomato relish.
Sweet Tomato Relish Combine ingredients in medium saucepan, place on barbecue; simmer, uncovered, until most of the liquid has evaporated. Cool. Remove and discard lemon grass.

SERVES 4
Per serving 15.9g fat; 1982kJ

lobster tails with
mustard sauce

10 kipfler
potatoes (500g)

4 small uncooked
lobster tails (620g)

2 medium limes
(160g), quartered

1/4 cup (70g)
seeded mustard

1/4 cup finely chopped
fresh chives

2 tablespoons white
wine vinegar

2 tablespoons olive oil

1 tablespoon
salmon roe

Boil, steam or microwave potatoes until just tender; halve lengthways.
Remove and discard soft shell from underneath lobster tails to expose
flesh. Cut each lobster tail in half lengthways.
Cook lobster, potato halves and lime wedges on heated oiled barbecue,
uncovered, until lobster is browned and cooked through and potato
and lime wedges are browned.
Whisk mustard, chives, vinegar and oil in small bowl; drizzle over
lobster, potato and lime, top with roe.

SERVES 4
Per serving 11.4g fat; 1316kJ

mini fish **patties**

with coriander yogurt

375g boneless white
fish fillets

1 tablespoon
oyster sauce

2 tablespoons finely
chopped fresh coriander

1 red thai chilli,
chopped finely

2 teaspoons finely
grated lemon rind

1 clove garlic, crushed

1 tablespoon grated
fresh ginger

3 green onions,
chopped finely

$^1/_2$ cup (75g) plain flour

cooking-oil spray

coriander yogurt

$^3/_4$ cup (210g) yogurt

1 clove garlic, crushed

2 tablespoons finely
chopped fresh coriander

1 teaspoon finely grated
lemon rind

1 tablespoon lemon juice

Blend or process fish, sauce, coriander,
chilli, rind, garlic, ginger and onion until
combined. Using floured hands, shape level
tablespoons of mixture into patties.
Coat patties with cooking-oil spray; cook
on heated oiled barbecue plate, uncovered,
until browned both sides and cooked
through. Serve with coriander yogurt.
Coriander Yogurt Combine ingredients
in small bowl.

MAKES 16
Per serving 1.2g fat; 227kJ

54 **crab** and prawn cakes
with salsa

750g large
uncooked prawns

500g shredded fresh
crab meat

1 red thai chilli, seeded,
chopped finely

1 teaspoon grated
fresh ginger

1/2 cup (75g) plain flour

**sweet chilli
cucumber salsa**

4 lebanese cucumbers
(520g), seeded,
chopped finely

1 medium red capsicum
(200g), seeded,
chopped finely

1/4 cup (60ml) sweet
chilli sauce

1 tablespoon fish sauce

1 tablespoon dry
white wine

1 tablespoon brown sugar

2 tablespoons finely
chopped fresh coriander

Shell and devein prawns. Blend or process
prawns, crab meat, chilli and ginger until
well combined. Using hands, shape
1/4-cup amounts of mixture into patties.
Cover; refrigerate until firm.

Just before serving, toss patties in flour,
shake off excess. Cook on heated oiled
barbecue plate, uncovered, until patties are
browned both sides and cooked through.
Serve with sweet chilli cucumber salsa.

Sweet Chilli Cucumber Salsa Combine
ingredients in medium bowl.

MAKES 12
Per serving 0.7g fat; 397kJ

mixed seafood
salad

500g medium
uncooked prawns

250g baby octopus

250g scallops

500g firm white
boneless fish fillets,
chopped coarsely

1/3 cup (80ml) olive oil

1 clove garlic, crushed

1 large red onion
(300g), sliced thinly

350g radishes,
sliced thinly

250g cherry
tomatoes, halved

1 medium green
capsicum (200g),
sliced thinly

250g baby
spinach leaves

**mustard yogurt
dressing**

3/4 cup (210g) yogurt

1 tablespoon
seeded mustard

1 tablespoon
lime juice

1 tablespoon water

1 clove garlic, crushed

Shell and devein prawns, leaving tails intact.
Remove and discard heads and beaks from
octopus; cut each octopus into quarters.
Combine prawns, octopus, scallops, fish,
oil and garlic in large bowl, cover; refrigerate
at least 20 minutes or until required.
Cook seafood on heated oiled barbecue,
uncovered, until cooked through. Gently
combine seafood in large bowl with onion,
radish, tomato, capsicum and spinach;
drizzle with mustard yogurt dressing.
Mustard Yogurt Dressing Whisk ingredients
in small bowl until combined.

SERVES 4
Per serving 24.6g fat; 2113kJ

raspberry vinaigrette

octopus

1kg baby octopus

2 cloves garlic,
crushed

1/3 cup (80ml)
raspberry vinegar

1/3 cup (80ml) olive oil

1/4 cup finely chopped
fresh oregano

Remove and discard heads and beaks from octopus. Combine octopus with remaining ingredients in large bowl, cover; refrigerate at least 20 minutes or until required.
Drain octopus over small bowl; reserve marinade. Cook octopus, uncovered, on heated oiled barbecue, brushing occasionally with reserved marinade, until browned lightly and tender.

SERVES 4
Per serving 20.7g fat; 1387kJ

butter sauce

4 snapper
fillets (800g)

2 tablespoons
lime juice

1 tablespoon
olive oil

2 teaspoons grated
fresh ginger

lime butter sauce

1/4 cup (60ml)
lime juice

1/4 cup (60ml) dry
white wine

125g butter,
chopped finely

pinch sugar

1 large egg tomato
(90g), seeded,
sliced thinly

1 tablespoon
finely shredded
fresh basil

Combine fish with remaining ingredients in large
bowl, cover; refrigerate at least 20 minutes or
until required. Drain fish; discard marinade.
Cook fish on heated oiled barbecue, uncovered,
until browned both sides and just cooked through.
Serve drizzled with lime butter sauce.
Lime Butter Sauce Combine juice and wine in
small saucepan, place on barbecue; simmer,
uncovered, until reduced to 2 tablespoons.
Gradually add pieces of butter, whisking
constantly until butter is melted (do not
allow sauce to boil). Remove from heat;
stir in sugar, tomato and basil.

SERVES 4
Per serving 33.2g fat; 2005kJ

58 asian-style

snapper in banana leaves

4 large banana leaves

4 whole bream or
snapper (1.5kg)

2 tablespoons grated
fresh ginger

1/3 cup (about 1 stalk)
thinly sliced fresh
lemon grass

2 cloves garlic, crushed

1 tablespoon
lime juice

2 tablespoons light
soy sauce

1/4 cup (60ml) sweet
chilli sauce

1 teaspoon sesame oil

1 cup (80g)
bean sprouts

225g baby bok choy,
chopped coarsely

2 trimmed celery
sticks (150g),
sliced thinly

4 green onions,
chopped finely

Cut each banana leaf into a 35cm square. Using tongs, dip one leaf at a time into large saucepan of boiling water; remove immediately, rinse under cold water, dry thoroughly. Leaves should be soft and pliable.

Cut fish three times on each side. Place each fish on a square of leaf; top with ginger and lemon grass. Combine garlic, juice, sauces and oil; drizzle a little mixture over each fish. Fold leaves over fish; secure parcels with kitchen string. Place parcels on barbecue, seam-side down. Cook in covered barbecue, using indirect heat, following manufacturer's instructions, about 25 minutes or until just cooked though.

Combine sprouts, bok choy, celery and onion with remaining sauce mixture. Cook on heated oiled barbecue plate, until just cooked and tender. Serve vegetable mixture with fish.

SERVES 4
Per serving 9.1g fat; 963kJ

glossary

bacon rashers also known as slices of bacon; made from cured, smoked pork side.

balmain bug a marine crustacean, this common species of slipper lobster (Ibacus peronii) has white flesh and a briny flavour.

banana leaves can be ordered, fresh and trimmed, from greengrocers. To trim further, cut with a sharp knife close to main stem, then immerse in hot water so leaves will be pliable.

barbecue sauce spicy, commercially made sauce used to baste or marinade, or as an accompaniment.

black beans fermented, salted soy beans; available in Asian grocery stores.

butter use salted or unsalted ("sweet") butter; 125g is equal to one stick butter.

cajun seasoning packaged blend of herbs and spices; can include paprika, basil, onion, fennel, thyme, cayenne and tarragon.

capers piquant grey-green buds of a shrub; sold dried and salted, or pickled. Before use: if salted, rinse and drain; if pickled, drain.

capsicum also known as bell pepper or, simply, pepper. Discard membranes and seeds before using.

chilli, red thai these are small, hot chillies.

crab
blue swimmer: also known as blue manna crab; when cooked, it turns red-orange and has sweet meat found in the legs and claws.
sticks: also known as seafood extender; processed seafood with a delicate flavour and no bones or wastage.

cream
low-fat sour: (minimum fat content 18%) commercially cultured soured cream; do not substitute for normal sour cream as it has a much thinner consistency.
light thickened: (minimum fat content 18%) ideal for use in sauces, soups and drinks.

eggplant also known as aubergine.

eggs some recipes in this book use raw or barely cooked eggs; exercise care if there are salmonella problems in your area.

fetta cheese Greek in origin; crumbly textured goat- or sheep-milk cheese with sharp, salty flavour.

fish sauce also called nam pla or nuoc nam; made from pulverised salted fermented fish. Has pungent smell and strong taste; use sparingly.

flour
plain: all-purpose flour, made from wheat.
self-raising: plain flour sifted with baking powder in the proportion of 1 cup flour to 2 teaspoons baking powder.

kecap manis also known as ketjap manis; Indonesian thick soy sauce which has sugar and spices added.

kumara orange-fleshed sweet potato often confused with yam.

lemons, preserved a North African specialty; lemons preserved in salt and lemon juice. To use, discard pulp, rinse rind; slice thinly. Sold in delicatessens in jars or bulk; once opened, store in refrigerator.

milk we used full-cream homogenised milk unless otherwise specified.

mirin sweet, low-alcohol rice wine used in Japanese cooking.

noodles, soba thin, spaghetti-like pale-brown noodle made from buckwheat and plain flour.

oil

cooking-oil spray: vegetable oil in an aerosol can.

olive: mono-unsaturated; made from the pressing of olives. Extra virgin and virgin are highest quality olive oils, obtained from the first pressings of the olives.

peanut: pressed from ground peanuts; has high smoke point.

sesame: made from white sesame seeds; a flavouring rather than cooking medium.

vegetable: any of a number of oils sourced from plants rather than animal fats.

onion

green: also known as scallion or (incorrectly) shallot; an immature onion picked before bulb has formed, having long, edible stalk.

red: also known as spanish, red spanish or bermuda onion; sweet-flavoured, large, purple-red onion.

oyster sauce rich sauce made from oyster extract, sugars, salt and other flavourings.

plum sauce a thick dipping sauce made from plums, apple, vinegar, sugar, chillies and spices.

potatoes, kipfler long and irregularly oval in shape, with yellow-tan skin and waxy, yellow flesh.

prawns also known as shrimp.

rocket also known as rucola, arugula and rugula; a fresh, green, spicy salad leaf.

sambal oelek (also ulek or olek) Indonesian in origin; a salty paste made from ground chillies and vinegar.

scallops a bivalve mollusc with fluted shell valve.

scampi also known as a langoustine; similar to a prawn but larger.

snow peas also called mange tout ("eat all").

spinach correct name for this leafy green vegetable; often called English spinach or, incorrectly, silverbeet. A small, or "baby", variety is also available.

sugar we used coarse granulated table sugar, also known as crystal sugar, unless otherwise specified.

brown: a soft, fine sugar retaining molasses to give it colour and flavour.

palm: very fine sugar from the coconut palm; sold in cakes, also known as gula jawa, gula melaka and jaggery.

sugar snap peas pods with small, formed peas inside.

tomato

puree: canned pureed tomato (not tomato paste).

sauce: also known as ketchup or catsup.

tortilla, corn thin, unleavened bread; purchase frozen, fresh or vacuum-packed.

wasabi an Asian horseradish having a fiery taste.

watercress has deep-green rounded leaves with a peppery flavour.

worcestershire sauce thin, dark-brown spicy sauce used as a seasoning and as a condiment.

zucchini also known as courgette.

index

artichoke, fish cutlets with 37
asian-style snapper in
  banana leaves 58
avocado mash, basil
  prawns with 31
avocado salsa, cajun
  seafood kebabs with 4
avocado sauce, creamy 33
bacon butter, oysters with 6
balmain bugs with oregano 8
basil prawns with
  avocado mash 31
black bean and chilli
  prawn kebabs 16
blue-eye with lemon
  and garlic 23
blue-eye, blackened, with sweet
  tomato relish 50
bream, walnut gremolata 34
bugs, balmain, with oregano 8
cajun orange roughy 15
cajun seafood kebabs
  with avocado salsa 4
caper dressing, sardines
  with tomatoes and 29
chilli ginger dipping sauce 32
chilli lime sauce, prawn
  kebabs with 36
chilli plum crabs 45
coconut prawns with
  coriander mayonnaise 11
corn husks, seafood 14
crab and prawn cakes
  with salsa 54
crab and zucchini fritters 7
crabs, chilli plum 45
cumin fish cutlets with coriander
  chilli sauce 48
devilled squid 12
dill and caper mayonnaise 33
dill caper cream 30
fish cutlets with artichoke 37
fish cutlets with salsa 28
fish cutlets, cumin,
  with coriander
    chilli sauce 48

fish patties, mini, with
  coriander yogurt 53
fish steak with tomato
  and chilli butter 26
flathead fillets with
  tarragon butter 17
fritters, crab and zucchini 7
garfish with leek, prosciutto
  and prawns 46
garlic prawns with
  tomato sauce 27
ginger tuna with wasabi
  drizzle 38
lemon and mustard
  squid hoods 42
lime and coriander
  octopus 35
lobster tails with
  mustard sauce 52
mayonnaise, coriander,
  coconut prawns with 11
mayonnaise, dill and caper 33
mayonnaise, pesto, salmon
  with kipfler potatoes and 40
mediterranean tuna steaks 44
mini fish patties with
  coriander yogurt 53
mussels, peppered herb 21
octopus, baby, salad 20
octopus, lime and coriander 35
octopus, raspberry
  vinaigrette 56
orange roughy, cajun 15
oysters with bacon butter 6
peppered herb mussels 21
pesto mayonnaise, salmon
  with kipfler potatoes and 40
prawn cakes, crab and,
  with salsa 54
prawn kebabs with
  chilli lime sauce 36
prawn kebabs, black bean
  and chilli 16
prawn sizzlers 49
prawns, basil, with
  avocado mash 31

prawns, coconut, with
  coriander mayonnaise 11
prawns, garlic, with
  tomato sauce 27
preserved-lemon yogurt 30
raspberry vinaigrette octopus 56
salad, baby octopus 20
salad, mixed seafood 55
salad, squid and watercress 24
salmon cutlets with creamy
  dill sauce 10
salmon with kipfler potatoes
  and pesto mayonnaise 40
salmon with two sauces 30
salsa, fish cutlets with 28
salsa, olive and fetta,
  tuna steaks with 43
sardines with tomatoes and
  caper dressing 29
scampi with fresh herbs 39
seafood corn husks 14
seafood kebabs, cajun,
  with avocado salsa 4
seafood salad, mixed 55
snapper with lime
  butter sauce 57
snapper, asian-style, in
  banana leaves 58
snapper, spiced, with
  nutty rice 18
snapper, teriyaki, with soba 13
squid and watercress salad 24
squid hoods, lemon
  and mustard 42
squid, devilled 12
thousand island dressing 32
tomato relish, sweet,
  blackened blue-eye with 50
tuna steaks with olive and
  fetta salsa 43
tuna steaks, mediterranean 44
tuna with vegetables 22
tuna, ginger, with
  wasabi drizzle 38
walnut gremolata bream 34

facts and figures 63

These conversions are approximate only, but the difference between an exact and the approximate conversion of various liquid and dry measures is minimal and will not affect your cooking results.

Note: NZ, Canada, USA and UK all use 15ml tablespoons. Australian tablespoons measure 20ml.

All cup and spoon measurements are level.

Measuring equipment

The difference between one country's measuring cups and another's is, at most, within a 2 or 3 teaspoon variance. (For the record, 1 Australian metric measuring cup holds approximately 250ml.) The most accurate way of measuring dry ingredients is to weigh them. For liquids, use a clear glass or plastic jug having metric markings.

How to measure

When using graduated measuring cups, shake dry ingredients loosely into the appropriate cup. Do not tap the cup on a bench or tightly pack the ingredients unless directed to do so. Level the top of measuring cups and measuring spoons with a knife. When measuring liquids, place a clear glass or plastic jug having metric markings on a flat surface to check accuracy at eye level.

Dry Measures

metric	imperial
15g	1/2oz
30g	1oz
60g	2oz
90g	3oz
125g	4oz (1/4lb)
155g	5oz
185g	6oz
220g	7oz
250g	8oz (1/2lb)
280g	9oz
315g	10oz
345g	11oz
375g	12oz (3/4lb)
410g	13oz
440g	14oz
470g	15oz
500g	16oz (1lb)
750g	24oz (1 1/2lb)
1kg	32oz (2lb)

We use large eggs having an average weight of 60g.

Liquid Measures

metric	imperial
30ml	1 fluid oz
60ml	2 fluid oz
100ml	3 fluid oz
125ml	4 fluid oz
150ml	5 fluid oz (1/4 pint/1 gill)
190ml	6 fluid oz
250ml (1cup)	8 fluid oz
300ml	10 fluid oz (1/2 pint)
500ml	16 fluid oz
600ml	20 fluid oz (1 pint)
1000ml (1litre)	1 3/4 pints

Helpful Measures

metric	imperial
3mm	1/8in
6mm	1/4in
1cm	1/2in
2cm	3/4in
2.5cm	1in
6cm	2 1/2in
8cm	3in
20cm	8in
23cm	9in
25cm	10in
30cm	12in (1ft)

Oven Temperatures

These oven temperatures are only a guide. Always check the manufacturer's manual.

	°C (Celsius)	°F (Fahrenheit)	Gas Mark
Very slow	120	250	1
Slow	150	300	2
Moderately slow	160	325	3
Moderate	180–190	350–375	4
Moderately hot	200–210	400–425	5
Hot	220–230	450–475	6
Very hot	240–250	500–525	7

at your fingertips

These elegant slipcovers store up to 10 mini books and make the books instantly accessible.

And the metric measuring cups and spoons make following our recipes a piece of cake.

Book Holder
Australia and overseas:
$A8.95 (incl. GST).

Metric Measuring Set
Australia: $6.50 (incl. GST).
New Zealand: $A8.00.
Elsewhere: $A9.95.
Prices include postage
and handling.
This offer is available
in all countries.

Mail or fax Photocopy and complete the
coupon below and post to ACP Books Reader
Offer, ACP Publishing, GPO Box 4967,
Sydney NSW 2001, or fax to (02) 9267 4967.

Phone Have your credit card details ready,
then phone 136 116 (Mon-Fri, 8.00am - 6.00pm;
Sat 8.00am - 6.00pm).

Australian residents We accept the credit
cards listed on the coupon, money orders
and cheques.

Overseas residents We accept the credit
cards listed on the coupon, drafts in $A drawn
on an Australian bank, and also British,
New Zealand and U.S. cheques in the
currency of the country of issue.

Photocopy and complete the coupon below

☐ **Book holder**   ☐ **Metric measuring set**
Please indicate number(s) required.

Mr/Mrs/Ms _____

Address _____

_____

Postcode _____ Country _____

Phone: Business hours ( ) _____

I enclose my cheque/money order for $_____ payable to ACP Publishing

OR: please charge $ _____ to my: ☐ Bankcard   ☐ Visa

☐ Amex   ☐ MasterCard   ☐ Diners Club   Expiry Date ___/___

Cardholder's signature _____

Please allow up to 30 days for delivery within Australia.

Allow up to 6 weeks for overseas deliveries. Both offers expire 31/12/02.
HLBS02

Food director Pamela Clark
Assistant food editor Kathy McGarry

ACP BOOKS STAFF
Editorial director Susan Tomnay
Creative Director Hieu Nguyen
Senior editor Julie Collard
Concept design Jackie Richards
Designer Caryl Wiggins
Publishing manager (sales) Jennifer McDonald
Publishing manager (rights & new titles)
Jane Hazell
Assistant brand manager Donna Gianniotis
Production manager Carol Currie

Publisher Sue Wannan
Group publisher Jill Baker
Chief executive officer John Alexander

Produced by ACP Books, Sydney.

Colour separations by
ACP Colour Graphics Pty Ltd, Sydney.
Printing by Dai Nippon Printing in Hong Kong.

Published by ACP Publishing Pty Limited,
54 Park St, Sydney; GPO Box 4088, Sydney,
NSW 1028. Ph: (02) 9282 8618
Fax: (02) 9267 9438.
acpbooks@acp.com.au
www.acpbooks.com.au

To order books phone 136 116.
Send recipe enquiries to
Recipeenquiries@acp.com.au

Australia Distributed by Network Services,
GPO Box 4088, Sydney, NSW 1028.
Ph: (02) 9282 8777 Fax: (02) 9264 3278.

United Kingdom Distributed by Australian
Consolidated Press (UK), Moulton Park Business
Centre, Red House Road, Moulton Park,
Northampton, NN3 6AQ. Ph: (01604) 497 531
Fax: (01604) 497 533 acpukltd@aol.com

Canada Distributed by Whitecap Books Ltd,
351 Lynn Ave, North Vancouver, BC, V7J 2C4,
Ph: (604) 980 9852.

New Zealand Distributed by Netlink Distribution
Company, Level 4, 23 Hargreaves St,
College Hill, Auckland 1, Ph: (9) 302 7616.

South Africa Distributed by
PSD Promotions (Pty) Ltd, PO Box 1175,
Isando 1600, SA, Ph: (011) 392 6065.

Clark, Pamela.
Barbecued Seafood.

Includes index.
ISBN 186396 245 X

1. Cookery (seafood).
I Title: Australian Women's Weekly.
(Series: Australian Women's Weekly
Make it Tonight mini series).

641.692

© ACP Publishing Pty Limited 2001
ABN 18 053 273 546

First published 2001. Reprinted 2002.

Cover: Prawn sizzlers, page 49.
Stylist Trish Heagerty
Photographer Scott Cameron
Back cover: Cajun seafood kebabs with
avocado salsa, page 4

The publishers would like to thank Bison Homeware,
Country Road Homewares, Ikea, Primo Imports
and Wheel & Barrow Homewares for props used
in photography.